SEARCH ENGINE OPTIMIZATION

The Advanced & Complete Step by Step Guide to Adult SEO and Backlinks

by Mike Triumph

The Advanced & Complete Step by Step Guide to Adult SEO and Backlinks

All rights reserved.

No part of this book may be reproduced in any form or by any electronic or mechanical means, including information storage and retrieval systems, without written permission from the author, except in the case of a reviewer, who may quote brief passages embodied in critical articles or in a review.

Trademarked names appear throughout this book. Rather than use a trademark symbol with every occurrence of a trademarked name, names are used in an editorial fashion, with no intention of infringement of the respective owner's trademark.

The information in this book is distributed on an "as is" basis, without warranty.

Although every precaution has been taken in the preparation of this work, neither the author nor the publisher shall have any liability to any person or entity with respect to any loss or damage caused or alleged to be caused directly or indirectly by the information contained in this book.

Enjoy it.

The Advanced & Complete Step by Step Guide to Adult SEO and Backlinks

Table Of Contents

What is SEO and what do you mean by Adult SEO?	5
Why would I want my website ranked higher in search results?	6
Why should I care about organic traffic from Google?	7
Who are you to explain about Adult search engine optimization, are you an expert or Guru?	7
Ok, I am convinced now, start teaching me SEO	8
Relevance of the page	9
Authority of the Domain	9
Authority of Inbound links	9
Relevance of inbound links	10
Majestic SEO	**10**
Moz Ratings	**10**
Basic SEO adult website set up	**11**
Rookie mistakes, beginner seo mistakes, newbie seo mistakes, and SEO traps to stay away from	**14**
Adult SEO Keywords – Queries, longtail – Get More Organic Traffic	**16**
Pornhub Keyword tool – Best keyword tool pornhub	**17**
What are Adult SEO keywords?	17
What are long tail keywords?	18
Optimizing your website for keywords and internal linking ?	18
Keyword Research For Adult websites	**18**
Adult Link-building strategy for adult seo	**20**

Method 1: Being a link detective	21
Method 2: Using comments and Forums	21
Method 3: Using link exchanges from relevant websites	23
Method 4: Using other not so great methods of link building	23
Method 5: Adding value and getting a link back	24
Method 6: Sponsored Posts or Paying money for links	25
Learn Adult SEO Understanding SEO for Adult Webmasters	**29**
Adult website – 301 redirect for Adult SEO	**30**
How to choose Porn seo, adult seo company, escort SEO companies and adult SEO services	**30**
What are Porn seo, adult seo , escort seo companies ?	31
That's great, why to worry when someone else can make me more money	31
I don't want to do SEO by myself, then how to choose the right company	31
Setting up payment terms your way	31
Ask them how are they are planning to improve your website rankings	32
Ask for client portfolio	32
Checking their Alexa rankings	32
Adult SEO Services by adult SEO company	32
Link-Wheeling for Adult SEO explained	**33**
What is Link Wheeling Adult SEO?	33

How can I do Link-Wheeling for Adult SEO on my websites?	33
How can I do internal link wheeling to pass on the page rank?	34
Adult SEO Tools for Adult webmasters	**35**
Avoid Over Optimization – Adult Seo and Backlink Building	**37**
Porn SEO trick that worked for me	**38**
List of Best free Porn image boards	39
Why you should avoid using Mobile Redirect Ads	40
Pinterest like Porn Pinning/Sharing websites for adult seo	40
Top 10 best ping sites for indexing and adult seo	42
Build adult backlinks using Who's That Pornstar sites	44
Selling and Buying Adult backlinks from SEOClerks explained	**45**
What is SEOClerks.com?	45
Do SEOclerks offer Adult SEO services?	46
Should I buy these services? Are these services legit? Is SEOclerks.com a scam?	46
How to buy adult traffic from SEOclerks?	47
How to buy adult backlinks from SEOclerks?	47
Can I become a seller? How can I sell digital marketing services on SEOclerks.com?	48
Adult Webmaster Resources – Ultimate List	49

Are you struggling to drive free organic traffic from Google to our website?

Are you finding it tough to do Adult SEO of your website and generate adult backlinks?

> Look at your site through the eyes of a user and stop worrying about spiders. Besides, Google only loves you if their users does.
>
> — *Mike Triumph*

The Advanced & Complete Step by Step Guide to Adult SEO and Backlinks

Worry not, today I will give you a step-by-step blueprint on how you can witness more than 500% increase in your visitors coming from Google in just 30 days. You just need to follow all the steps given here on this article.

If you are searching for Adult SEO, pornhub keyword tool, adult SEO company, adult SEO service or in general porn SEO then you have the right guide.

With more than 10+ years experience in building adult websites and teaching SEO, I know what I am talking about. So make sure you take the time and read through this guide, follow it, reread it and have fun!

Organic traffic is the best way when you are searching for how to promote adult site?. I have done it multiple times on more than 30+ of my adult websites, ranging from webcam models, adult blogs, selling porn clips, escort website, and hundreds of clients websites as well. This is a best way to make a decent amount from online business.

This article is an Advanced Guide to Adult SEO and adult Backlinks. I will try to cover almost all the things that works and what you must also do to supercharge your adult website. I will first explain what SEO (search engine optimization) is and then will tell you how it has changed over the years. I will also cover recent trends, working techniques, methods, tips, tricks to drive extensive organic traffic to your adult website.

Search engine optimization is the best form of adult website marketing in my opinion.

This book will be beneficial to you if you can identify yourself with any of the following:

The Advanced & Complete Step by Step Guide to Adult SEO and Backlinks

1. Curious to learn about SEO.
2. Webcam model/camgirl/adult performer/pornstar/clipstore studio or model/Escort/adult escort website.
3. Adult seo company and companies providing adult seo services.
4. Adult webmaster.
5. Owner of any kind of adult website.
6. Adult affiliate marketer or into adult affiliate.

Note: This advanced guide is long, so try to grab as much as possible, if you are new to SEO then try to read it multiple times to understand everything correctly.

What is SEO and what do you mean by Adult SEO?

This is how Wikipedia defines SEO. SEO stands for Search Engine Optimization, and hence the goal of SEO is to optimize your website in such a way that your website is ranked higher in search results of major search engines like Google, Bing etc. (Although we will only focus on Google, as majority of market share is occupied by them).

Adult SEO is no different from normal SEO, however, the link building process (which I will talk about later) is a little different. The best part about building adult backlinks and driving traffic is that the competition is comparatively much lower and hence ranking websites is easier. Before moving forward with teaching you how to do adult SEO of your website, you need to first understand how SEO works, and hence I will first be explaining the basic cores and fundamentals of SEO to you

The Advanced & Complete Step by Step Guide to Adult SEO and Backlinks

Why would I want my website ranked higher in search results?

The higher the ranking, the more number of visitors your website will get. According to data, 50-60% people click on the first result of a search query, 20-25%o on the second search result and only 8-12% on third search results. So you can imagine if your website is on second page of Google, then probably no one will be coming to your website for the target search query.

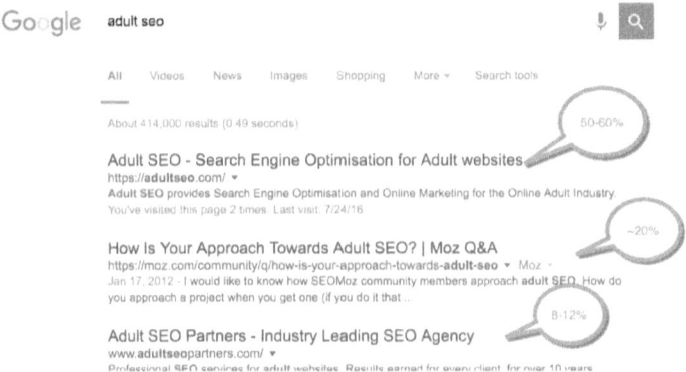

Why should I care about organic traffic from Google?

The answer is simple, its free and targeted. Let me explain each point in detail:

1. Free traffic: Since you are not paying to drive traffic to your website, people are finding your website on the platform of Google and coming to your website. You don't have to spend any money to drive those visitors to your website. Once you are on top in search result then you will get huge traffic.
2. Targeted traffic: This is very important. If your website is about selling guitars, but the people coming to your website are interested in buying a mobile phone, then no one will stay on your website for long. When people are coming to your website from Google, they are searching for something that your website has to offer and hence when they land on your website they are more likely to purchase what you have to offer. Google only ranks those website to a particular search query that has content related to that search term. Google is very strict about their policy.

Whenever someone has a website, the most important metric is the traffic your website gets. The more the traffic, the more money you will make, whatever be the niche you are in. If you are not utilizing the power of Google then most probably you are missing out on a big opportunity.

Who are you to explain about Adult search engine optimization, are you an expert or Guru?

The Advanced & Complete Step by Step Guide to Adult SEO and Backlinks

Let me clear up something first, I am no guru or an SEO expert. But I have been building websites for more than 20 years now (10+ years in the adult industry) and the majority of my traffic comes from Google for almost 50+ websites I have (making me more than $10,000/month). I love to learn and have learned from the experts in the SEO industry, I have purchased many too expensive SEO courses to learn as well. Also, all the techniques I will be mentioning later are being performed on my websites as well, hence I can guarantee they work. Because they works for me as well. If I can do it, so can you man!

Here is a snapshot of one of my website, as you can see approximately 70% of my traffic comes from Google, all this happened just because I followed these SEO techniques.

Default Channel Grouping	Sessions	% New Sessions	New Users
	584,494 % of Total 100.00% (584,494)	74.52% Avg for View 74.30% (0.28%)	435,536 % of Total 100.28% (434,306)
1. Organic Search	393,238 (67.28%)	74.36%	292,430 (67.14%)
2. Direct	184,214 (31.52%)	76.22%	140,399 (32.23%)
3. Referral	6,628 (1.13%)	36.00%	2,386 (0.55%)
4. Social	404 (0.07%)	79.46%	321 (0.07%)
5. (Other)	10 (0.00%)	0.00%	0 (0.00%)

Ok, I am convinced now, start teaching me SEO

Great lets start with your adult SEO training and how you can also drive enormous adult traffic for your adult website. Here are the Goals of SEO:

And how do we do this: Google looks at what is on the website, Google then looks at the links that are coming into the site, Google then gives certain links more power than others. In a nutshell, the most relevant site with the most powerful adult backlinks coming in wins the race and is awarded the highest search engine rankings

The most important Four points in your Adult SEO campaign will be:

- Relevance of the page
- Authority of the Domain
- Relevance of inbound links
- Authority of Inbound links

Lets Go through each point one by one.

Relevance of the page

This comes under on-page Adult SEO. This basically is how relevant the page you are trying to rank is with the search query. The points that matter are:

1. **Title of the page:** Make sure your target keyword is in the title of the page.
2. **Titles of the image:** Images should have "ALT TEXT" which includes the keywords that you are targeting.
3. **The content of the page:** The content must be at least 500 words and properly optimized for the keyword that you are targeting.
4. **Videos of the page**: Having a relevant video increases authority of the post.
5. **Description of the page:** Keywords that you are targeting must be in the description of the page.
6. Other On-page factors.

Authority of the Domain

This factor is harder to emulate as this cannot be done overnight. It takes the time to build domain authority (DA). A number of factors affect domain authority such as:

1. The links pointing to the domain name.
2. The number of unique high-quality SEO optimized pages/posts on your website.
3. Social factors (social traffic, CTR (click-through rates) and other social signals)

Authority of Inbound links

This is one of the most important factors and we will be covering this in detail throughout the post. Adult backlinks are the key factors that will help your website rank higher and push your website in front of thousands of people. There are many blackhat ways to build thousands of adult backlinks within one day, but all that will do to your website is get penalized. The most important thing is to make high-quality adult backlinks. Focus on Quality vs Quantity. When it comes to the authority of links, following points should be kept in mind:

1. Inbound links or the backlink to your website.
2. Power of the pages where are inbound link is present.
3. Power of the domain where the inbound adult backlink is present.

Relevance of inbound links

This factor has always be ignored by most of the webmasters that are struggling with getting their websites ranked higher in Google. If your website is about selling Guitars, but majority of your adult backlinks are coming from websites that are totally unrelated to guitars like Dog food, computer peripheral etc, then the power of that backlink is significantly reduced. You would want the adult backlinks to come from related domain niche, such as guitar training, guitar schools etc. Relevancy is the key to high quality adult backlinks.

These were the top four factors that you need to consider before going forward with your adult seo training and building high quality adult backlinks. I have list of four amazing SEO tools, that will help you improve SEO of your website, they are trusted by millions of people, and are considered to be the best tools by SEO experts:

1. Majestic SEO (Accurate and Simple):
2. MOZ (Best representation of Authority)
3. Ahrefs (most links counted, but sadly a paid tool)
4. SEMrush (similar tool with great power)

The two key tools we will be using are:

Majestic SEO

Trust Flow and Citation Flow are calculated. Trust flow is the best representation of authority of the website. You must be targeting those websites that have a Trust Flow and Citation flow with a ration of 1:1, this indicates that the website is high quality. You would also want the trust flow to be at least **10.**

Moz Ratings

The Advanced & Complete Step by Step Guide to Adult SEO and Backlinks

First, I will recommend you to install the Moz bar. Domain authority and page authority are good measures when coupled with Trust flow to get the profile and authority of any website.

Note: Moz misses a lot of adult backlinks and hence the number of adult backlinks and the sources of these adult backlinks will not be the complete profile, for that I will recommend using Majestic and Ahrefs.

Before continuing further, let me tell about one few more important tips and tricks that you can use to optimize your post and website.

Basic SEO adult website set up

You must install "Yoast SEO" plugin (WordPress) for your website and it will automatically tell you how to optimise your page is. Let me first also cover other important on-page adult SEO factors that you need to focus on.

Let me explain to you how you can use internal linking to rank pages of your website and how internal linking can easily optimize your website. If you look at the above stated bullet points then those are internal links of other posts on this website. Internal linking is a great way of passing link juice between pages. Here is an image to explain this better:

By creating relevant pages or supporting pages and then pointing to the main page you are trying to rank is a great way of adult seo. In this image, the arrows are a representation of from where the link juice is getting transferred to the target pages. If all the pages are pointing to a single page, then it indicates to Google, that this page has something important to offer, also the link juice is getting passed and hence that target page starts to rank higher on search results.

Adult friendly domain name

It is highly recommended to have your focus keyword in your domain name. Google gives special ranking benefits to such websites. Although this feature has been consecutively abused by people, but I have been doing the same for my new websites and its still working. Try not to make the domain name exact as the focus keyword, rather add a helping word to avoid getting blacklisted.

High Quality content
I have emphasize on this point multiple times, because this is one of the most important area of your website. In this highly competitive worked of online websites, to be able to stand out of the crowd you need to offer enormous value to the reader from your website. A website visitor has many options when he is looking for some information, for him/her to become a fan of your website you need to give him exactly what he wants and even more.

Here are some pointers to keep in mind.

1. The content must be unique.
2. Dated articles must be updated. Things change everyday, so a 1-year-old article might not be useful today, so update it with relevant information.
3. Interlinking relevant articles. Give them a reason to stay long. Interlink articles on your website so that the visitor stays for a much longer time.
4. Add articles on a regular basis. A regularly updated website is crawled multiple times by Google and given preference in search engine rankings.
5. Make it an easy read. Use friendly and engaging language. Add media (pictures, videos, gifs etc.) to elaborate and explain in a much better way.
6. Don't write small 200-300 words articles. Try to write at least 600 words in each article. (Note: Do not add irrelevant information if your article is of lesser words, always remember add as much value as possible.

Adult Seo optimizing your article or post

The Advanced & Complete Step by Step Guide to Adult SEO and Backlinks

After writing your high quality article/post, you need to optimize it for search engines. I hope you are using WordPress CMS for your website. Install Yoast SEO and try to get green light. Follow all the recommendations it says and fulfill them all. This plugin alone will help you a lot in you on-site adult seo optimization. You can add custom keywords for each and every page or posts.

Leverage the visitor for Seo and more traffic
A high quality article which can have a positive affect on the visitor if more likely to be shared by him/her. So make a call-to-action in order to make him share the article on social media platforms. Commenting on the articles can also help a lot.

Submitting the Sitemap to Google
Using Google Webmaster to submit the sitemap. Google webmaster will be your got place for chaching your website ranking on Google- the leading search engine.

Generate the sitemap of your WordPress website using this plugin : BWP sitemap

Adding keyword rich site title and tagline
Adding the focus keyword of your niche or website in site title also helps in seo benefits and is a good seo strategy. Add relevant additional important keywords in site tagline.

Keyword friendly Article/post Permalink
Having the focus keyword in the urn of your articles is also very important. So make sure that the keyword you are targeting is shown in the url structure of your articles

Highlighting or making the keywords bold
Make sure to highlight, italic or bold the keywords in your articles to get that extra seo benefit.

Adding Alt tags to images

Any image you upload to your website can be adult seo optimized by adding the focus keyword of that article/post as alt tag of the image. This will help drive additional traffic from image search engines. Also this will improve overall seo score of the article/post.

Website speed is a very important parameter
Do not miss this step. This is highly critical; a fast loading website is given special preference over a slow website. Also I saw a jump in multiple website rankings when I improved the speed of my website.

Tip: Try to get the Data Center, or your server close to the country where majority of your traffic is coming from. For example, if 80% of your traffic is coming from United States, then getting a US server will be extremely beneficial.

Rookie mistakes, beginner seo mistakes, newbie seo mistakes, and SEO traps to stay away from

Let me cover the mistakes that you can make while doing search engine optimization of your website. Learning from other people's mistakes is the best form of learning and today I will cover exactly what you should not do for your adult website link building.

1. Thinking this SEO stuff is so complex and giving up – Don't do that, path to success is not easy my friend.
2. Focusing on quantity vs quality, One high quality backlink is much more powerful than 100 crappy adult backlinks my friend.
3. Building too many backlinks too quickly – this will alert google about something fishy and you might get a penalty, and trust me recovering from a Google penalty is very tough.
4. Buying links, using black hat methods of link building, indulging in link farms, link pyramids, etc – Dont even think about these stuff.

Another beginner mistake is to not consider the "Nofollow" links. Nofollow adult backlinks are those that do point to your website or page, but do not pass the link juice and hence are not considered by Google. Newbies think since they are not helpful to rankings they don't build them, but trust me they are important as well. The trust flow metric also considers "Nofollow" links to build the authority of the website. Also Google might be alert if the website only has "doFollow" links as that might not look natural. Even social signals are all "nofollow" links but Google gives weightage for social signals for rankings.

Let me also cover Mobile Responsiveness: Since you all know that the world is shifting to mobile. More and more websites are witnessing an ever increasing mobile users. Facebook themselves have accepted that their mobile users are so many times higher then desktop users. Google has been giving ranking benefits to mobile-friendly websites, by this they mean:

1. Fast loading website on mobile.
2. Responsive design, easily adaptable to any mobile screen and hence increased user experience.

You must have also seen on Google search results that the websites that are optimized for mobile (mobile friendly website theme) has a small "mobile-friendly" written along the search result. So make sure the theme of your website is responsive and easily adaptable with every screen size, if you are purchasing a theme from platforms such as ThemeForest, then you don't need to worry about it as the developers are making mobile friendly themes now. I have noticed a sudden increase in my traffic on one of my website when I switched to a mobile-friendly them.

Staying Away from PBN's: PBN (Private blog network) was earlier used by many people to rank their website on Google, it is just like a link farm and total black hat way of gaining SEO rankings. It is highly unsafe to buy links from PBN's and Link farms. Although many experienced SEO experts know how to use them the right way, but as an amateur SEO person you should stay away from them. You have never use the black hat link binding techniques.

Adult SEO Keywords – Queries, longtail – Get More Organic Traffic

Lets discuss over Adult SEO Keywords – Queries, longtail – Get More Organic Traffic. Keywords are the most important criteria you choose to optimize the posts that you add to your website. Google checks your website for specific keywords to give a ranking to your website on its search results. Finding, targeting and then optimizing your adult website for the right keyword is surprisingly important.

Pornhub Keyword tool – Best keyword tool pornhub

If you are searching for pornhub keyword tools then trust me you won't find a genuine product, because there is no such thing as pornhub keyword tool. Its really amazing tool for searching the keywords.

The best ways to find adult keywords or pornhub keywords is to use tools like Semrush and Ahrefs and then either use their own keyword tools for finding search volume of popular keywords like "porn" etc. You can also put the ranking URL (no#1 position) into [a hrefs] and then find out about how much organic traffic is driven to this link and which keywords are driving that traffic.

Porn SEO is not that difficult if you know your tools right and also if you follow this guide conscientious.

What are Adult SEO keywords?

One thing you have to understand is that the primary goal of Google is to offer the best and the most relevant article on the first result for any search query. I the end the primary purpose of Google is to provide the information that the person is looking for. If that person is able to find that information in the first link itself, then the purpose of Google is served. Google always try to find the relevent articles with the search keywords on different websites.

Keywords are a way google get to know a little about the content of your article. Apart from other adult seo factors, Keywords is like a deliberation of your website in the eyes of google.

The Advanced & Complete Step by Step Guide to Adult SEO and Backlinks

If you website is about *Blowjob*, then queries and keyword such as "*Blowjob videos*" is a keyword. You target is to rank on number one spot of search results for this search query. If your website have the same or relevent keywords then it will be indexed on the Google Search.

Finding the right keywords in not enough, you then need to optimize your website and article according to the keywords you are targeting.

What are long tail keywords?

Because of increased competition on the internet, and thousands of websites being opened in almost every niche, it has become extremely difficult to outrank already established websites for certain keywords. For example, you will find Wikipedia articles on majority of general topics as first search result, and it is very difficult to out rank those article, so you have to target the long tail keywords.

Lets say someone is searching for "blowjob video girl sucking big cock abc studio", this is an example of long tail keyword. Since with just "*blowjob videos*" , already thousands of website is targeting that keyword because of its high search volume, you can target longtail keywords to get that additional traffic with less competition. The only drawback is that very few people are searching for those queries. But if you have a website where you are selling affiliate products, even few extra sales can make all the difference. Also ranking higher for long tail search keywords is comparatively much easier.

Optimizing your website for keywords and internal linking ?

You will have to think like the person searching the query. What is going on in their mind when they are making a query on Google. If you can crack it and you just have to put all the relevent search query keywords wiht articles on your website.

People generally search for pornstar names, or the studio names that are producing these porn videos. So adding internal links to the tag or category page of these porn stars or studios from each individual post will drive them higher in search rankings.

Keyword Research For Adult websites

Keyword Research Adult sites or finding adult keywords, one of the most essential and important step, which decides your success in making money online through adult websites. Finding the right keywords can directly affect your online money making capabilities.

Finding the right keywords for your website is not that hard. Although there are paid tools available but even the free ones will do the job. I will list both the paid and free tools available on the internet that can help you create a comprehensive keyword list.

Let us first start with the Free adult keyword finding Tools.

Google Keyword planner

A free tool, coming directly from the big daddy of search engines. The name is Google. You can find Googles Keyword Planner right here!

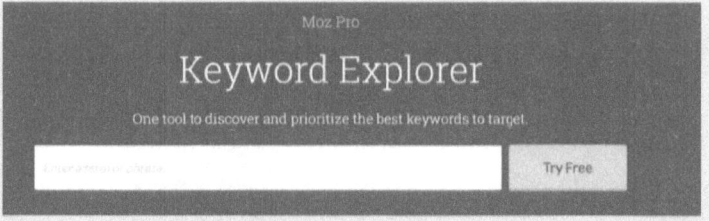

MOZ keyword Explorer adult keywords

This is somewhat limited free edition. You can make two free search queries and then you will be asked to pay. The tool tracks your IP address for free searches, so install the Zenmate Browser, Browsec addon for changing the IP address and making multiple free searches. I like this tool, because apart from Google Keyword planner, many more addition keywords can be found on Moz keyword Explorer.

Once you have the excel sheet then you can remove the duplicate keywords from the keywords column to just have the unique keywords. The Keyword Research Adult sites will give you a long list of adult keywords to target. You just need to remove the duplicate keywords use the conditional formatting:

Finding keywords, the hard way

One of the strategy that I apply to find the right keywords I looking at my competitor's keywords. What are the keywords he is targeting, what kind of articles/post he is making on his/her website? Spending some time on this tactic will help you a lot as well.

These three techniques will themselves help you create a huge lust of keywords to target. If you want to dig deep and look at other important parameters like:

1. Competitiveness of the keyword to rank on Google.
2. A detailed analysis of keywords your competitor is targeting.
3. Find long tail keywords in your niche.
4. Find more related keywords.

Then you will need to buy a paid service. There are few amazing services and software's on the internet. I ones I will recommend that will benefit you the most is:

1. Market Samurai.
2. SEMRUSH Pro
3. Long tail pro.

Although if you just want to invest in only one service, go with Serums. It is market leader in keyword analysis and getting your website ranked on Google

Adult Link-building strategy for adult seo

Let us start with adult back-links strategy. I will be covering a lot of ways and methods on how you can start link-building for your adult website. Let me first give you the pros and cons of adult backlink building:

Here are the advantages you already have:

1. **Low competition:** Compared to other normal websites, adult websites are comparatively easier to rank because competition is way less.

Here is the disadvantage you have:

1. **Lack of link opportunities:** Finding backlink opportunities (especially high quality ones) is really very difficult. As normal websites do not want to link themselves with adult websites and hence you have limited resources to build adult backlinks.

Let me list down the ways of building a link profile for your website one by one.

Method 1: Being a link detective

Although there are great many ways of link building for normal non-adult websites, but when it comes yo adult the opportunities are very less. One of the best ways to make backlinks is to fist find opportunities by checking the link profiles of your competition.

The Advanced & Complete Step by Step Guide to Adult SEO and Backlinks

Step-1: Make an excel sheet (here you will copy all the links of the places you will be making backlink on later).

Step-2: Use tools like majestic, https://www.ranksignals.com (free tool) for looking at backlink profile of your competition. For every link check the Trust flow, and Domain authority if you find a good backlink opportunity then copy the link in your excel sheet. You should check the link profile of at-least 8-10 of your competition.

Using this method alone you will find hundreds of places from where you can build adult backlinks.

Method 2: Using comments and Forums

Although this method has been heavily used for ages now and hence Google has stopped giving it much appropriateness. You must not spend much of your time on building comments adult backlinks at least.

TIP: One very important tip I can give you is to not use "Anchor text' for your adult backlinks when using comments and Forums. Since these links has gotten a negative implication when it comes to link building, always paste the direct link for the page that you are targeting. Using anchor text will highly increase the chances of Google penalty.

Here is a list of search commands you can use to find relevant comment opportunities:

1. keyword "1 comment"
2. keyword "2 comments"
3. keyword "3 comments"
4. keyword "4 comments"
5. keyword disqus
6. keyword "leave a comment"

For forums you can use:

1. keyword"forum"
2. keyword"powered by Fireboard"
3. keyword"powered by ip.board"
4. keyword"powered by phpbb"
5. keyword"powered by phpbb3"
6. keyword"powered by SMF"
7. keyword"powered by vbulletin"
8. keywordforum
9. keywordintitle:forum
10. keywordinurl:forum

Method 3: Using link exchanges from relevant websites

You might have seen this on many adult websites where they list a number of websites in a widget with title "Our Friends" . This helps them getting adult backlinks from relevant websites in their niche. You can easily make a list of websites in your domain and contact them though email for link exchange. Make sure no one will link to you if your website traffic is not comparable to the one you are trying to get a link back from.

TIP: Make sure you check the trust flow and Domain authority of the website you are trying to get a link from. You would not want to link to a website which is spammy or low quality.

Method 4: Using other not so great methods of link building

These methods were working great earlier or few years back, but now they don't work that much. But building links through these techniques will help you diversify your link profiles and help your link building look more natural. I have written several articles on this here o this website:

The Advanced & Complete Step by Step Guide to Adult SEO and Backlinks

There are many places to build backlinks. First let me give to a checklist of what you must do and must keep in mind.

1. Vary your anchor text.
2. Build adult backlinks of all quality (33% low quality, 33% moderate quality, 33% high quality)
3. Only make maximum of 3-5 adult backlinks in a day.

Remember one very important thing. Google has changed its algorithm and now they want the backlink to come from a website that is in the same niche or related niche of your website. So make 50% of your backlinks from the websites that are in your niche.

Method 5: Adding value and getting a link back

This is more like a smart strategy, also this might not work will all types of adult websites. But this method requires some work from your end hence you will have to do some hard work but the links you will get are surprising. Let me give you an example, don't you like it when someone helps you without any ill motive or expecting something in return, this is what we will be exploiting in this method. In this method you will be going through the websites in your niche, help the owner of the website in one way or another, and then ask them for a link to your website.

Remember: If you get a "Anchor Text" link well and good, but even if you were able to get a direct url link even that has some power to boost your rankings.

Here are the steps that you need to follow:

The Advanced & Complete Step by Step Guide to Adult SEO and Backlinks

1. Make a list of all the websites that are in your niche
2. Sort the websites in terms of the quality of website and the power of backlink you will get. (use tools such as MOZ and Majestic for ranking the website, you can use the metric of Trust flow to rank the websites)
3. Start going through each website and look for any one of the following:
    - Broken links on the website (giving 404 response) (use browser plugins for this).
    - If the content is outdated, and you have the knowledge of updated content.
    - Deleted videos if it is a tube website (make a list of at least 50 of the deleted videos on that website)
    - If the website is extremely slow or the user experience is pathetic. You must increase the loading time of your website.
    - Any other type of value that you can add to the website owner.
4. Draft an email and add the value in your email and send it to each website.
5. Do the above steps for as many websites as you can , also make sure you keep a column for contact information (either contact form url or if direct email is available).
6. Once the website owner sees the email and thanks you for helping him, you can then tell them about your website and how it is related to the same niche as their website. 9 times out of 10, they will be happy to link back to your website.

The motive here is to help other person first and then ask for something in return. By adding value first you were able to win his trust and then he/she will be highly likely to link back to you. Just make sure the link is "dofollow".

Method 6: Sponsored Posts or Paying money for links

The Advanced & Complete Step by Step Guide to Adult SEO and Backlinks

Sponsored posts should be your last technique of link building. Let me also tell you that they come under BlackHatways of adult backlinks building since we are paying to get our links on other peoples website. If you read earlier in this article I asked you to stay away from buying links (I was talking about PBN's and link farms) , but sponsored posts are still a safer and more effective method that buying links because they are real, active, clean sites that just happen to make money from advertisers (Just like Inc, Forbes etc).

Note 1: This method can get expensive, generally depending on the quality of the website, you might have to pay in between ($30-$300) per post, but mostly in ~$100 range. Worry not I will tell you about negotiation techniques.

Note 2: Make sure you do extensive research on the quality of the link – make sure that it is not a link farm.

Our goal will be to look for websites that are looking for a monetization method, and hence by offering them some money in exchange of a Link is mutual benefit. So make an excel sheet and fill it with websites that are related in your niche – blogs, tubes, etc. Also make sure you make a column for contacting them either through contact form, but email is preferred

Before contacting them do the following checks:

1. Domain authority and Trust flow
2. Content quality(are they indulging in spamming)
3. Do they "nofollow" the sponsored post or not

Negotiating the price: Keep one thing in mind, that the person you are contacting need the money more than you think. So tell them honestly that the prices they are asking is out of your budget and then give them a reason why they should lower the price. 9 times out of 10 they will come up with a lower price.

I understand that the number of websites wont be large as the niche is adult in nature, but you also have to understand that since the competition is not that high, even few links will be really helpful in driving the rankings of your website high up in the search engines.

Other tips:

Getting adult backlinks from Websites and Blogs

One most important thing to keep in mind is, get links from website which are in your niche. Relevant websites are the only ones that you must be targeting for your backlinks.

Here are the steps:

1. Make a list of websites in your niche. (These are your competitors)
2. Since the websites are on same niche and targeting the same keywords, the strength of the backlink will be huge.
3. Email them through their contact form about your website and how both can benefit from link trade
4. Usually a link is placed in the right widget or footer as "friends of xyz.com".

Remember if you are just starting out then don't expect the big players in your niche to link to you. The best way is to target the website who are almost equivalent to your level of traffic.

Getting social media links

Google has mentioned that they give some weightage to social signals. So if your articles or posts are getting shared on the social media platforms a lot, then this will directly help you in SEO rankings in search engine results. Google give you special benefit of social sharing.

You can automate this process by using a website like Hootsuite.com. Also there are plugins which automatically post your recently published article automatically to your social media accounts.

Also make sure to add Call-to-action, asking your website readers to share your content on social media platforms. Remember people will only share content they loved. This will only happen when you write high quality content in your website.

One problem you might face is that not all social media platforms allow adult content. The ones that do is:

1. Tumblr
2. Reddit
3. Twitter
4. AdultNode

For other platforms like Facebook, be wary of the guidelines and post only stuff that will not get you banned.

Adult Directories and link pyramids

If you have followed my other adult seo guides for porn sites, then you know how much I hate these spammy link building techniques. Google will instantly blacklist your website when they find your website indulging in this shady blackhat ways of backlinks building. Instead of helping you in SEO they will negatively affect your website rankings.

Even if you spot an adult directory in your niche, prefer quality over quality. Stay away from spammy adult directories.

Using email list for adult backlinks building and adult seo

Email list is a critical tool if you are an adult performer (clip store studio owner or camming model). If you own an adult tube website, then creating a mailing list wont really help you a lot.

Email list can be utilized in several ways.

1. Building stronger relationships with your followers.
2. Creating a community, which is an essential part of a website.
3. Adding more value to your subscribers.
4. An available audience to promote anything
    1. Don't misuse this feature. First add a lot of value in their life, and only then you can request them or drive them to something that you want for yourself.

So how can you do adult seo using email list?

You can give a freebie (like and eBook or any other thing) in exchange of asking them to share your content on their social networks. You can even create a content locker, where the content will only be available when someone follows certain stenos like.

1. Liking on Facebook Page
2. Following on twitter
3. Sharing the article on their twitter timeline

Most Important TIP: It is very important that you spend quite some time on Adult SEO and link building. Initially I thought that i will add some high quality content and easily organic traffic will start flowing in my website. I was wrong, you need to build a link profile, and indulge in adult seo if you are serious about your website and want to make some significant income from them

Learn Adult SEO Understanding SEO for Adult Webmasters

The videos are distributed by Google itself, so this gives us guarantee that it works. high quality Google Webmaster videos on their YouTube channel, is the ultimate source of understanding Search Engine Optimization.

Most of the ideas feature Matt Cutts, One of Google's software engineer. He heads the Google search team. I have listed the videos in order of how you should view them. I will request you to watch each episode with full attention, once you understand how SEO works you can then easily relate and help your adult website grow faster.

Videos can be seen on their Youtube Channel.

Adult website – 301 redirect for Adult SEO

Now I will tell you about 301 redirect for Adult SEO if you own an adult website.

In the adult tube website methods you might need to remove some post for some reason or another. One of the most common problems for adult tube website owners is that users upload content that is not owned by them. You must use your own content. The copyright owner will then send a DMCA removal request to your email id.

You are required to remove the contravene url or post on your website within few days, otherwise legal actions might be taken against you. When you remove the infringing url then you also lose the traffic that was being generated by that post. Let us assume that particular post got many backlinks and was helping in adult seo of your website. In such case removing the post will also remove any seo benefit that your adult website might be getting because of that post. You have to remove that post from your website and this is not good for you.

To solve this problem all you have to do is that instead of removing the post do the following steps:

1. Instead of removing/deleting the post, just convert the post from published to Draft status. This way the post wont be live on the website.
2. Install the WordPress plugin 301 redirects.
3. Now just the url of that post and paste it in the "Request" section. And the paste the homepage on your destination url.
4. This way Google will transfer the SEO benefit from that post to your homepage.

How to choose Porn seo, adult seo company, escort SEO companies and adult SEO services

The Advanced & Complete Step by Step Guide to Adult SEO and Backlinks

Today is a very important topic: How to choose Porn seo, adult seo company and adult seo services, escort seo companies. If you own an adult website be it:

1. Become a Webcam model
2. Escort Website
3. Adult video selling
4. Become a Porn Star
5. Adult services

Then sooner or later you will be contacted by so called adult seo company to help you get better rankings on Google.

What are Porn seo, adult seo, escort seo companies?

Just like any online business, the better rankings you have for your target keywords the more free targeted customers you will receive. Since you are selling a service or product, better Google rankings will directly affect your earnings ad profitability. This is what are the advantages by these adult seo companies to sell their service to you. They promise to give you Top rankings on your target keywords.

That's great, why to worry when someone else can make me more money

Honestly SEO is a road which only few people understand. Most of these so-called escort seo, porn seo or adult seo companies are run by amateur who are looking to make quick dollars. They might even know what works in search engine optimization and will end up hurting your website by doing black hat techniques of link building. If you have read my articles on this website:

Then you know the right and best way to do seo for your adult website.

I don't want to do SEO by myself, then how to choose the right company

Well let me give you the best ways to choose the right adult seo company for your adult business.

Setting up payment terms your way

Instead of giving flat payments rather the payments will be result driven. If you are currently ranked on 20th place for your target keyword, make sure you only pay incremental, like if you are jumping up by one position you give 5% of the money and so on.

If they hesitate when you talk about such payment arrangement, that means they are not authentic/re-putative company.

Ask them how are they are planning to improve your website rankings

If they use black hat methods , or offer hundred of backlinks within few days that means they don't know what they are doing. This will give you a basic idea of what to do and what not to do in your SEO strategy. This way you will be easily make judgement about the authenticity of the company. You must have to choose the one who know all the tips and tricks of white hat SEO link buildings.

Ask for client portfolio

If the company is genuine, they will be happy to share their client portfolios. You can then easily contact any other client for the review of this SEO company. If they are hesitating in showing their client portfolio that means something fishy is going on.

Checking their Alexa rankings

Although there are black hat ways to boost the Alexa rankings, but this is a good metric of checking the traffic of these company website. If the Alexa ranking is more than 1 million, that means the company is stay or just a newbie in this market.

Adult SEO Services by adult SEO company

If you are also searching for an adult seo company then pause your search, follow the instruction of this adult seo guide and if you still don't see results then hire a reliable adult seo services company. Trust me you will save lot of money this way. You will save lot of time as well. I have done adult industry seo for 7+ years now, and what I am sharing with you in this guide it works.

Link-Wheeling for Adult SEO explained

If you know a little bit about Link wheeling method of building adult backlinks, then you probably know that it is looked upon with a shady eyes. With recent Google algorithm updates, it is considered to be a blackhat way of building links. The issue was that people started spamming and without giving a thought about the right method of creating backlinks, in the end got Google penalty.

What is Link Wheeling Adult SEO?

Link wheeling is another way of creating high quality adult backlinks for your website to improve Adult seo of your website. When you own many domain names and then you link them to each other in the form of dofollow backlinks, it is called linkwheeling.

The best part about Link wheeling way of doing adult seo is that all the websites benefit since they are sharing the link juice with each other, and hence get even more organic traffic because of improved rankings.

If you are in adult industry then you would have seen this methods of building links to a website on almost every other adult website. Especially in adult tube websites, it is a very popular way of building adult backlinks.

How can I do Link-Wheeling for Adult SEO on my websites?

The Advanced & Complete Step by Step Guide to Adult SEO and Backlinks

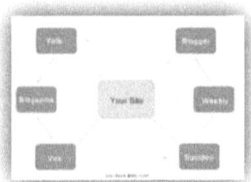

I wrote an article about this on how you can ask other adult websites in your niche to include your website link the sidebar. These sitewide links are an especially amazing way to share link just also drive additional traffic to your website. Check the article here: Make Adult backlinks using Link exchange website.

Note: With increased scrutiny from google, you must keep in mind that the sitewide link is exchanged between the sites that are in similar niche, if your website is about Blowjob, then try to exchange links only from blowjob based websites. Also, since you are linking to a site in the same niche, the traffic trade also helps in getting more relevant targeted visitors.

How can I do internal link wheeling to pass on the page rank?

One technique I use on my adult tube website is to do internal link wheeling on my website. Lets say that there is a pornstar names "abc" and I have more than 100 videos of that pornstar on my website. So what I will do is create an internal link to the tag page of that pornstar from each individual video post of that pornstar on the website. This was that tag page is improved in the rankings of Google and hence more traffic is sent from google. Also, since most of people are generally searching for a video or a pornstar using queries such as "*abc videos*" etc hence that tag page will then rank higher for such search queries.

Adult SEO Tools for Adult webmasters

Adult SEO Tools for Adult webmasters are extremely condemnatory in helping you become successful in online adult industry. A smart adult webmaster knows his industry and told that can maximize his chances of making money. There are multiple amazing free tools available online that can really have a drastic impact on your journey of making money. You can be in any of the following industry:

1. Adult tube websites
2. Webcam model/cramming model/adult performer personal website
3. Adult blog
4. Review Blog
5. Adult products company
6. Adult services company
7. Dating blog
8. Any other adult related business

Google Webmasters Tools

A free tool by the search giant Google himself. Google webmaster will give you a full report of your website seo performance of the search engine.

1. Keywords and the ranking of your website for that keywords
2. Graph of how your website is performing on different keywords
3. Click through rate, impressions, etc.
4. Websites issues
   - Broken links
   - Sitemap problems
   - Malicious content on your website
   - Website being blacklisted
5. How your website is being crawled by web spiders?
6. Health of your website.

Google Analytics

Another free indispensable tool, that will tell you everything about

1. An overall in-depth information about your visitors
2. Geography of visitors
3. Bounce rate, page views, pages/visit
4. Traffic sources
   - Organic traffic
   - Referral traffic
   - Direct traffic
5. Conversion rate, how much of your traffic converts
6. Behavior of your traffic on the website
7. Million other things
8. Browser or technology they use

Honestly listing all the amazing features of Google analytics is impossible, a must has free adult seo tool for any adult webmaster.

Google keyword planner

Finding the right keywords for your website is extremely important. This free tool helps you find the right adult keywords.

Free trial of MOZ SEO tool and Ahrefs

Take the free trial of these two website seo tools, to understand almost everything about your niche. You can always cancel, just google the name + free trial and you can get started. They will show you:

1. Your website analysis
2. SEO profile of your website
3. Backlink opportunities
4. Competitor analysis
5. Keywords you can target
6. And much more

The big daddy of SEO, MOZ has written an amazing article covering almost 100 amazing tools that can help you make smart decision and make your life easier. Check the article out 100 free seo tools.

Avoid Over Optimization – Adult Seo and Backlink Building

Adult Seo can be a little tricky when compared with general SEO techniques. Because the content here is not general its an Adult, so most of search engine do not support the adult content. Although the methods remain the same, but not all the websites accept adult content thereby creating a problem for adult webmasters.

The Advanced & Complete Step by Step Guide to Adult SEO and Backlinks

If you witness a sudden drop in your website visitors or traffic, then you might have suffered from a Google penalty. It is extremely hard to recover from a penalty, hence I advise you to follow some guidelines to prevent yourself in the first place.

However sometimes, unaware people indulge in **SEO over optimization** and suffer from Google penalties and losing all the visitors and hard work. This article will cover the best practices to follow so that you are safe and insusceptible from any Google penalties and get quality search engine rankings.

Adult SEO is a complicated game and one needs to learn by trial and error what works and what doesn't. Both on-page and off-page factors are considered by Google's spiders when crawling a website. I will be listing down some key points, which I have learned over years of being into adult industry. Follow these SEO practices:

1) Do not use black hat or any other unethical adult link building techniques.

2) Avoid grammatical errors, spelling mistakes in your content.

3) Keep the keyword density below 7%.

4) Stay away from duplicate content, write your own original high quality content. Your content must be unique and effective.

5) Do not ever link to spam websites, link farms, or any other shady place of link exchange. Few quality backlinks are worth more than thousands of worthless links.

6) Avoid keyword stuffing, or rather do not overdo it (on post, page and domain).

7) Never try to trick or fool the search engines, sooner or later it will backfire.

8) Do not try to make thousands of adult backlink on a daily basis, link building should look natural and hence devote one hour everyday and only make quality backlinks. As the website starts getting more traffic then you can increase the number of links you make per day. It is all about looking natural in the eyes of Google.

9) Do not buy gigs, which promise tens of thousands of backlinks in few days. You will lose both the money and your website rankings.

10) Do not waste your time building no-dofollow backlinks, as they wont be considered by Google for ranking your website.

When a search engine websites crawls a website, it looks at many different parameters to rank your website in comparison to others in your competition. If you follow quality SEO methods then sooner or later you will start ranking higher for your chosen focus keyword.

Porn SEO trick that worked for me

I don't know why it works but it has been giving me amazing results for last three years. I found this trick by chance. This gives my website initial attention that you needs of Google. When you just start your website its very difficult to get noticed. There are already many established websites in your niche and they are the ones that get recommended by google in the search results.

These beginning days of you website are the most difficult once. You barely get traffic and you do everything to increase it to a acceptable level.

The Advanced & Complete Step by Step Guide to Adult SEO and Backlinks

Once when I was creating a tube website, instead of focusing on building backlinks like I used to do, I just started doing tube uploads with branding to let the people come back to my website. What this did was people started typing the domain name of my website on Google and then traffic started pouring in. The best part about this traffic was that since the traffic is targeted, the bounce rate was only close to 20-25%. That must have given a strong signals to Google that this website has something of great value to offer.

Once I stopped my tube uploads, I could see that I started ranking for related keywords in my niche without even building any backlinks.

So, just because people came to my website after searching my domain name on Google and stayed there for a very long time, that helped me in my Adult SEO a lot. I am not sure why this trick works, or the reason I am assuming is right or wrong, I just know it works. Let me show you a screenshot of what I am trying to say:

As you can see, after tube uploads I saw a great influx of traffic and within a week in my Google Webmaster I could see many search queries for which I was ranking at not so bad positions.

List of Best free Porn image boards

I have compiled this List of Best free Porn image boards to help everyone who is trying to supercharge his adult seo by building backlinks and optimizing the website.

The Advanced & Complete Step by Step Guide to Adult SEO and Backlinks

- Anon-IB
- 7Chan
- iChan
- **Porn-Chan**
- 4Chan
- WetChan
- XXXChan

Why you should avoid using Mobile Redirect Ads

I have been in adult content making money business for almost four years now and I can assure you that you should **completely avoid Mobile redirect ad type in your website.** The reason being why send your valuable hard earned visitors to some other website when those precious visitors can be channelized to give you much more ROI (Return on Investment) when they visit your own website.

- Firstly there are chances that the visitor might get irritated by going to some other website, so there is a high probability of loosing a repeat visitor.
- Secondly you never know, that one particular visitor might end up buying a affiliate product or joining a Cam sight that you are promoting and thereby earning you much more than what you were earning through mobile-redirects
- Thirdly and most importantly, Google has started penalizing websites with mobile redirects, so if you are ready to lose only SEO advantage then its your call in the end

If you are one of those stubborn person and thinks that what i say is crap, then you may try this ad platform for yourself. Or if you have loads of traffic but not making much money from traditional advertisements then you may try mobile-redirect ad platform. The best network that provides the best rates for mobile redirect ads is Plugrush.

The Advanced & Complete Step by Step Guide to Adult SEO and Backlinks

Pinterest like Porn Pinning/Sharing websites for adult seo

If you are also tired of searching google about **SEO for adult websites** or a **list of porn pinning websites** with not even a single blog or website that can guide you on **how to rank a adult website on #1 position on google.** Well then your search ends here. As you already know one of the key component for adult seo is backlinks but the problem lies in the fact that compared to white hat seo, **creating adult backlinks** is a much more tougher task.

Today I will give you a list of Pinterest like Porn Sharing websites for adult SEO. Creating these backlinks wont take you more than two hours and within few weeks you will see 20-30 backlinks pointing towards your website.

Here's a screenshot of the backlinks from these websites after I created them for one of my newly made adult tube website (just to show and prove all those who thinks that this will never work):

The Advanced & Complete Step by Step Guide to Adult SEO and Backlinks

Here is the **list of porn pinning websites**:

1) Sex

2) Smutty

3) PunchPin

4) Zmut

5) Porn4Free

6) The Free Fap

7) Smuttaroo

8) LustPin

9) Sex Social Pin Board

10) Fapp

11) Jerk Pin

12) HD Porn Photos

13) Porn Pin It

14) Pin Faps

15) Porno Pin

16) Porn Pin

17) Smut Pin

Note: Let me tell you beforehand that majority of these websites are pinterest clones and please do not expect **high quality adult backlinks**.

Top 10 best ping sites for indexing and adult seo

Ping websites are an amazing way to let major search engines (like Google, Yahoo, Bing), blogs and directories know about your website and also asking them in an indirect way to index your website and its pages. Pinging a blog or a website (especially a new one) is like shouting in a high pitch voice about the availability of your website.

Pinging a website is extremely easy and does not require you to be a Adult Seo guru. All you have to do is to submit the domain name or URL of your website and click the submit button, these ping websites will handle the task of informing the major search engines about your adult website. Creating adult backlinks is hard and pinging is an easy and effective way to get your adult website (or a normal website) get indexed super fast and thereby helping you with your Adult SEO campaign.

The Advanced & Complete Step by Step Guide to Adult SEO and Backlinks

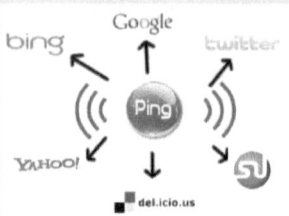

How will pinging help your website:

- Indexing your website in key search engines and directories in very short time.
- It also might help in creating some backlinks.
- Increasing the visibility of your website in search engines.
- It also helps search engine know about any changes or updation in your websites.

Here is the list of **Top 10 best ping sites for indexing and adult seo and adult backlinks:**

- Pingomatic.com – Pagerank 6
- Twingly.com – Pagerank 6
- Auto-ping.com – Pagerank 5
- Blo.gs – Pagerank 5
- Feedshark.brainbliss.com – Pagerank 5
- **Mypagerank.net** – Pagerank 5
- Icerocket.com – Pagerank 5
- Bitacoras.com – Pagerank 5
- Totalping.com – Pagerank 4
- Ping.in – Pagerank 4

Build adult backlinks using Who's That Pornstar sites

The Advanced & Complete Step by Step Guide to Adult SEO and Backlinks

Build adult backlinks using Who's That Pornstar sites. Making high quality adult backlinks for your adult website is one of the toughest issue that an adult webmaster or an adult website owner faces. Although I have covered almost all the techniques related to building adult backlinks, there are still many ways to build adult backlinks, one of which I will be sharing today.

Adult backlinks are the key factor that affects the adult seo of your website. Please check Adult seo guide article to find all the relevant article on this website that will help you get massive organic traffic from Google.

I will be sharing one more technique of building adult backlinks today using "Who's That Pornstar" sites. Just like Porn pinning sites, Who's That Pornstar sites are a platform where general audience can show a picture or a link of a video to ask others about the pornstar name. People can then reply to that question with the name of the pornstar and much more information.

How can this technique be used to build adult backlinks?

There are two ways you can build adult backlinks using this technique. Either you yourself ask question by first sharing a link towards your website and then people can reply to that question.

This method of creating adult backlinks, is used by very few but this is an amazing way to create high quality adult backlinks.

Sometimes, your website audience also might share the video link of your website on such Who's that pornstar website inquiring about the pornstar name in the video.

Where can I find a list of "Who's That Pornstar" sites?

The Advanced & Complete Step by Step Guide to Adult SEO and Backlinks

To help our adultaffiliateguide.com visitors, I have compiled a list of all the websites which offers a platform for asking questions regarding pornstar name:

1. Namethatporn.com
2. Namethatpornstar.com

There are many similar websites, but these two are the most popular ones.

Selling and Buying Adult backlinks from SEOClerks explained

I receive countless emails and messages on Facebook asking me how to build quality adult backlinks.

Few desperate souls, get attracted by the easy way of buying adult backlinks from websites like SEOclerks.com, thinking magically their search engine rankings will improve. SEO has always been a much debated topic and understanding the correct way to accomplish it takes time. Let's talk about buy/sell adult backlinks and traffic from seoclerks. If you dont want to read the whole article then you can directly signup using the following link: Signup SEOclerks.

What is SEOClerks.com?

This website is focused on people and companies, that sell their SEO services for money. Key services offered are boiling backlinks of your website and driving traffic to your website. Apart form beige an SEO marketplace, you can even buy tweets, articles, blog reviews, EBooks, software's and themes.

If you are a newbie and have no clue about doing SEO of your website, then this website can be helpful in getting you started. You can easily buy affordable seo services and help the google rankings of your website.

The Advanced & Complete Step by Step Guide to Adult SEO and Backlinks

Do SEOclerks offer Adult SEO services?

Yes, apart from general website SEO services, seoclerks also offers adult seo and backlinks services. You wont find all the services offering adult backlinks as well, but you will need to find the right guys that also offer adult seo. Doing a simple search with "Adult" can also help you find adult seo services.

Should I buy these services? Are these services legit? Is SEOclerks.com a scam?

If you have been following my website, then you know that I am strictly against using any SEO services or any link building services. I rely on building my website slowly and steadily. Anything that offers amazing Google rankings within days or weeks looks shady to me.

SEO is something that should be taken seriously and should be handled delicately. Google is not a fool, they keep changing their algorithms, so that no one has the power to affect their Google rankings within days.

I will be honest; I remember I have bought few adult seo services myself from SEOclerks.com. Fro one of my niche adult tube website (which was not getting enough traffic and rankings even after spending a lot of time and energy), I bought a couple of services. Honestly, I did see the backlinks being built in the Google Webmaster links section, but did not witness any significant change in my Google rankings.

I am not being only negative about this website. In few of the forums, I have seen trusted people (adult webmasters) achieving good results from SEOclerks. Maybe I was unlucky with seoclerks.

My advice will be to find the trusted services. A lot of black hat techniques and methods are also being used by few services for see of your website. This will negatively impact your website. So be careful before choosing the service and paying the money. You don't want any scammer to just create some spam my links in exchange of your hard earned money.

How to buy adult traffic from SEOclerks?

Getting traffic, it your website is tough. It takes time, commitment, patience and hard work. Yes, you can pay money to get traffic to your website, but then again in the end you must get a positive ROI (Return on Investment) to do so. Yes, there are many sellers that offer real adult niche traffic for very cheap prices. But then again you need to be wary of the quality of these services. After finding the service that you can trust, start small and spend only few dollars to test this service. If you find that the traffic is real and of quality, then you can ask for more traffic.

SEOclerks world seems very attractive, if seems as if all your problems can be solved for few dollars. I agree, but keep in mind nothing of high quality comes cheap. Make smart decision instead of foolish one.

How to buy adult backlinks from SEOclerks?

Just like adult traffic, buying adult backlinks is on top priority of adult webmasters or porn site owners. Although I have always suggested to follow my ADULT see section to build adult backlinks, but if you are in a hurry then you can try their adult backlinks service. Keep the following points in mind:

The Advanced & Complete Step by Step Guide to Adult SEO and Backlinks

1. Only go for trusted sellers.
2. Try to stay away from services offering very high gains for very few dollars, these are spammers and will make spammy links (services like Build 10,000 adult backlinks for $5)
3. Understand the basic of ADULT seo before buying such services.
4. Do not directly go for complete website SEO, rather first buy few backlinks and test their quality.

Can I become a seller? How can I sell digital marketing services on SEOclerks.com?

If you are not looking for services buy rather offering your services, then you can also register as a seller. If you already have an adult website, social media account, or Expert SEO knowledge then you can easily offer your services for a small fee. There are multiple services that you can sell on SEOclerks.com:

1. **Sell high quality adult traffic on SEOclerks:** You can either divert the traffic to client's website using banner ads, popups, social media traffic generation (Tumblr, reedit, twitter etc.). One great way to make money is being an amazing adult media buyer. If you know how to buy cheap but high quality traffic, then you can sell that for a higher price. Let's say you can generate 10,000 visitors for $20, then you can easily sell that service of $30 or more.
2. **Build adult websites on SEOclersk :** I am assuming that you already know how to build a porn site or adult website and make money off it. Then why not sell these services on SEOclerks. If you have been following y website, then you already know a lot about making money through porn or adult content. There are a lot of different services that you can sell like crating a niche based adult tube website, finding right keywords for your adult website, optimizing the adult website, make more money from adult website etc.
3. **Make money from your adult social media accounts:** An amazing way to make money from your popular or high following social media accounts on platforms like Twitter, Tumblr, Instagram is to seal sponsored post. People will pay you money to talk about them in your social media account. The bigger the following you have, the bigger the reach and hence higher the fees. You can also sell your social media account to prospective buyers.
4. **Sell adult backlinks on SEOclerks:** People will pay anything for some high quality adult backlinks. Already creating den building adult backlinks is difficult. SO if you are able to create few good quality backlinks from your existing adult websites then you can charge a fees for that. You can charge for different time period like monthly, quarterly, yearly or for lifetime and keep different fees for each. You can easily find clients for adult backlinks.

I have covered a lot in this article, now its your time to start investing in your website and make decent passive income.

Adult Webmaster Resources – Ultimate List

The Advanced & Complete Step by Step Guide to Adult SEO and Backlinks

This Adult Webmaster Resources – Ultimate List will cover all the tools, softwares, websites you need in order to become successful. As an Adult webmaster you need a variety of information. The best part about internet is that there are so many amazing tools out there that can make the job of an adult webmaster extremely easy.

Although i have tried to cover all the Adult Webmaster Resources, but i am not an expert. If you think that i have missed a resource, or you know about something which might benefit us all, please do share in the comments section below.

Most of the tools listed here are free. Some might have a free offer with an option to upgrade to Pro version.

Domain and Adult Friendly Hosting

1. Hostgator is 100% needed to get solid hosting

Website data – Traffic, Statistics etc

1. SEMrush
2. Google Analytics
3. Google Webmaster

WordPress plugins for your adult websites

1. JWplayer
2. Wp-rocket or W3 Total Cache
3. WP Smush
4. Search Meter
5. Better WordPress Google XML Sitemaps
6. Add to All
7. Simple 301 Redirects
8. UpdraftPlus – Backup/Restore
9. WordPress Editorial Calendar
10. WP-Optimize
11. Yoast SEO

Additional Helpful tools for your adult website

1. Cloudflare.
2. Speed test websites (https://tools.pingdom.com/ , https://gtmetrix.com/ , https://developers.google.com/speed/pagespeed/insights/)

Adult Affiliate Networks

1. CrakRevenue

Tools that are helpful in creating creatives for Adult Media Buying

1. Adobe Photoshop.
2. Snagit.
3. Any image compression tool.

Best Adult Advertisement Networks

1. Juicyads
2. Exoclick
3. Popcash
4. ExocitAds

First of all congratulations for reading this entire article. I hope this article was helpful and now you have a direction about yoru adult website.

That's it! You've reached the end! I hope you liked this e-book! If you have any questions please feel free to send me an e-mail at any time: hi@miketriumph.com

Thank you so much for reading! Now go make some money! Spend that time and put in the work. For every hour you watch TV or stream a stupid show, spend 3 hours working on your online projects so you can reach your dreams.

Remember: If I can do it, so can you! I'm just an average guy man!

Love.

Mike T.

Do the work Stay Focused

Ever wonder why some people "make it" and others don't? Sure some are born with a big fat golden spoon up their ass, but that's less than 1% of us. The fact remains, that most of us are just average working people trying to get by.

So why do some rise to the top? Why do some make a ton of money online and others do not? I will tell you why. They have awesome work ethics and they maintain focus!

They aren't binge streaming the latest show on Netflix, Hulu or Disney. They work. They grind and they focus.

What does that have to do with this e-book you ask? Nothing and everything! It has everything to do with SUCCESS and if you bought this PDF (or stole it) and read to this very last page, I really want you to succeed and make a lot of fucking money!

So stay focused, do the work and put in the time until you reach your magic number. For me it was $10K/month. What's yours?

Mike Triumph

www.ingramcontent.com/pod-product-compliance
Lightning Source LLC
Chambersburg PA
CBHW020623220526
45463CB00006B/2655